# More Good Choices, Bad Choices

Jean Stapleton

10 9 8 7 6 5 4 3 2 1

Copyright © 2020 Jean Stapleton
Paperback ISBN: 978-1-5271-0528-7

Published by Christian Focus Publications,
Geanies House, Fearn, Tain, Ross-shire,
IV20 1TW, Scotland, U.K.
www.christianfocus.com;
email: info@christianfocus.com

Cover design by Daniel van Straaten
Cover illustration and page layout by Daniel van Straaten
Printed in Turkey by Imago

All rights reserved. No part of this publication may be reproduced, stored in a retrieval system, or transmitted, in any form, by any means, electronic, mechanical, photocopying, recording or otherwise without the prior permission of the publisher or a licence permitting restricted copying. In the U.K. such licences are issued by the Copyright Licensing Agency, 4 Battlebridge Lane, London, SE1 2HX. www.cla.co.uk

Scripture taken from the New King James Version. Copyright © 1982 by Thomas Nelson, Inc. Used by permission. All rights reserved.

# CONTENTS

Introduction .................................................................5
The Four Lepers: A Daring Choice ..................7
Jehoshaphat: The Good King who Made
 a Disastrous Choice ....................................10
Jehoiada and Jehosheba Made a Courageous
 Choice ............................................................13
Joash makes an Evil Choice............................16
Uzziah: The King who Chose to act like a Priest...18
Ebed-Melech who Chose to Stand up
 for God's Prophet .........................................21
Jonah: The Reluctant Prophet's Choice................... 24
Daniel: The Young Man's Choice....................27
Three Young Men who Chose not to Bow Down ..... 30
Daniel: The Governor's Choice ...................... 33
Queen Vashti's Choice .....................................36
The King's Choices and the Choice
 Mordecai Made ............................................ 38
Haman's Choice and Queen Esther's Choice.... 40
King Ahasuerus Makes Some More Choices............ 42
Nehemiah: The Cupbearer's Choice............................ 46
The King who Chose to Destroy Little Children...... 49
The Pharisees: The Religious Leaders' Choice ........ 52
Nicodemus: The Pharisee who Chose
 to meet Jesus ................................................. 55

The Four Friends: A Determined Choice ................. 58
John the Baptist's Brave Choice............................ 60
The Man who Chose to Speak the Truth ................. 63
Two Sisters: Two Choices............................................ 66
The Ten Lepers: Different Choices............................ 69
The Rich Young Man's Choice................................... 71
Zacchaeus: Who Chose to do Right ..........................74
A Widow's Choice to Give Everything ..................... 76
The Centurion who Chose to Believe ..................... 79
A Woman's Two Choices: When Sick
 and When Healed ...................................................... 81
Mary's Loving Choice.................................................. 83
Judas: A Terrible Choice............................................. 86
Pilate: Who Chose to Please the People................... 89
The Secret Disciple who Chose to Come Forward .. 92
Thomas who Chose to Doubt..................................... 95
Peter and John Choose to Obey God......................... 97
Ananias and Sapphira: A Dishonest Choice .......... 100
Saul: Who Chose to Persecute Christians............... 103
Felix: Who Chose to Procrastinate .......................... 106
King Agrippa: Who Almost Made a Right Choice ..108
Julius: The Centurion's Choice to save Paul ...........111
The Most Important Choice: Revelation 22:17 ...... 113

# INTRODUCTION

In this second book about choices, we look at some more Old Testament characters and then move on into the New Testament. The Bible tells us about these people, so that we will learn from their experiences and from the consequences of the choices they made (1 Corinthians 10: 11).

The Bible had many human authors, but God's Holy Spirit helped each one to write His messages to us (2 Peter 1: 21). As you read each day, ask God for help from that same Holy Spirit, so that you will understand and remember what you read. Remember too, to ask God to help you, whenever you have a choice to make.

Jean Stapleton

**Dedication:**
**To Beryl who thought about choices**

# THE FOUR LEPERS: A DARING CHOICE

The city of Samaria was besieged by the Syrian army. As time went by, there was no food left and the people were in great distress. The king of Israel blamed the prophet Elisha for their trouble. Elisha said that on the next day, there would be plenty of food.

The northern kingdom of Israel did not have any kings who were obedient to God. When their disobedience brought trouble on the land, more than once it was the prophet who was blamed. The prophet was the one person who had told them the truth about themselves.

At the city gate there were four men who had leprosy. At that time, lepers had to live separately from other people. They knew that if they did nothing, they would starve to death. The lepers decided that they would surrender to the Syrian army. The Syrians might keep them alive, but if they were killed it would be no worse than starvation.

A surprise awaited the four lepers. There was no one in the Syrian camp. God had caused

the Syrians to hear a noise like a great army and they had fled leaving all their possessions behind. The four lepers went into a tent and had food and drink. They then began to take things for themselves: silver, gold and clothing.

Suddenly the four men realised that they had another choice to make. Should they go on taking things for themselves or should they tell the good news to others? They knew that they must make sure that the king knew what they had found. They called the gatekeepers of Samaria and they passed on the news to the king's household.

At first the king thought that the Syrians were tricking them, to draw them out of the city. He sent men to see whether the Syrian soldiers were hiding somewhere. They found no one, only the things the soldiers had dropped as they fled.

The people of the city soon made their way to the Syrian's camp. They found plenty of food, as Elisha had prophesied.

## READ: 2 KINGS 6:24-25; 7:1-16
## QUESTIONS:
1. What was the first choice that the four lepers made? (2 Kings 7:3-4)
2. Why had the Syrian army fled? (2 Kings 7:5-7)
3. What was the second choice the four lepers made? (2 Kings 7:8-9)

# JEHOSHAPHAT: THE GOOD KING WHO MADE A DISASTROUS CHOICE

Jehoshaphat was a good king who loved and obeyed God. He took away idols that had been set up in the land of Judah and he sent men to teach God's law to the people. He became powerful and none of the nations around Judah tried to attack him. However, there came a time when Jehoshaphat made a wrong choice.

In the northern kingdom of Israel there was a very wicked king named Ahab. Living in days when parents arranged marriage for their children, Jehoshaphat's son, Jehoram, was married to Ahab's daughter, Athaliah. Ahab and his wife, Jezebel, worshipped a false God called Baal. Athaliah had grown up with idolatry and could not be a suitable wife for the person who would become the next king of Judah.

It was after Jehoshaphat's death that the results of his wrong choice took place. His son, Jehoram, became king and encouraged the people to worship idols. This was because his wife, Athaliah, brought the idolatry of Ahab and

Jezebel into Judah. Jehoram reigned for eight years, but became seriously ill and died. His son, Ahaziah, was king for one year and was killed.

Athaliah, the widow of king Jehoram, killed her own grandchildren (Ahaziah's children) so that she could become queen over Judah. So the people of Judah had a woman reigning over them who was cruel and idolatrous.

It is sad to think that Jehoshaphat who really loved God, could have made a foolish choice that resulted in such terrible events in the land of Judah. But God never forgets His promises. He had told King David long before, that there would always be a king from his family. The aunt of Ahaziah's sons whose name was Jehosheba, managed to save Ahaziah's youngest child, Joash, who was just one year old. Jehosheba was married to Jehoiada the priest. They were able to keep Joash hidden in a room in the temple for six years. When Joash was seven years old, Jehoiada proclaimed that he was the rightful king of Judah. Athaliah was put to death for the evil she had done.

The story of Jehoshaphat reminds us that even a person who loves God and does many things that are right, can sometimes make wrong choices. It also teaches us that no foolish choice, no evil woman, can prevent God keeping His promise to His people.

### READ: 2 CHRONICLES 17:1-10; 18:1-3; 19:5-7; 21:5-6; 22:2-4; 10-12
### QUESTIONS:
1. What good things did King Jehoshaphat do for the people of Judah? (2 Chronicles 17:6-9; 19:5-7)
2. What was the wrong choice that he made? (2 Chronicles 18:1)
3. What terrible events resulted from Jehoshaphat's wrong choice? (2 Chronicles 21:5-6; 22:2-4; 10-12 )

# JEHOIADA AND JEHOSHEBA MADE A COURAGEOUS CHOICE

Athaliah was an evil woman. She was the daughter of King Ahab of the northern kingdom of Israel. Ahab worshipped idols and when Athaliah married the son of Jehoshaphat, king of Judah, she brought idolatry with her. After her husband died, her son, Ahaziah, became king. After he also died, Athaliah chose to carry out an evil plan. She would kill all those who could be made king of Judah – her own grandchildren. Then she would reign as queen over the land.

In the days when David was king of Israel, God had promised that there would always be a king from David's family. Could God's promise be broken because of an evil woman? God had two people who were faithful to Him and ready to make a courageous choice.

Jehosheba was the sister of King Ahaziah, the aunt of the children that Athaliah had decided to kill. Jehosheba was not able to rescue all the children, but she did save the youngest one, one-year-old Joash. Jehosheba was married to

Jehoiada, the priest. Together, they hid little Joash in a room in the temple. They kept him hidden for six years. When they did this, they were choosing to act in a very courageous way. They would have known that if Athaliah had found out what they were doing, their lives would have been in danger, as well as the life of the little prince.

For six years Jehoiada and his wife kept their secret. For six long years those who trusted in God must have wondered about God's promise. Then, when Joash was seven years old, Jehoiada again decided to act courageously. It was time for the people to know that the true king of Judah was alive.

Carefully, Jehoiada made his plans. All the Levites were called to the temple. The armed guard was set up and the leaders of the people brought together. Joash was then brought to the temple and crowned king.

Athaliah heard sounds of music and singing and came to the temple. She actually shouted "treason" as if she was the rightful queen. Jehoiada gave instructions and she was taken out and put to death.

## READ: 2 CHRONICLES 22:10-12; 23:1-21
## QUESTIONS:
1. What was Athaliah's evil plan? (2 Chronicles 22:10)
2. What was Jehoiada and Jehosheba's courageous plan? (2 Chronicles 22:11-12)
3. What did Athaliah hear? (2 Chronicles 23:12-13) and what did she see? (2 Chronicles 23:13)

## JOASH MAKES AN EVIL CHOICE

It is wonderful to think of how one-year-old Joash was saved from wicked Athaliah. He was hidden for six years by his uncle and aunt, Jehoiada the priest and his wife, Jehosheba. When Joash was crowned king over Judah, he was only seven years old. It was Jehoiada who taught him what he ought to do. Jehoiada lived to be a very old man but after he died at 130 years of age, things changed.

Some of the leading men of Judah came to speak to King Joash. The king listened and began to join them in worshipping idols. Now Jehoiada had a son whose name was Zechariah. God gave Zechariah a message for the people. He stood up and spoke to them about how they were disobeying God's commandments. He told them that because they had turned away from God, God would no longer be with them to help them.

The people did not like what Zechariah said. Joash told them to put Zechariah to death. He was stoned to death in the temple courtyard.

Joash had ordered the death of the son of the man who had helped him more than any other.

Joash forgot all Jehoiada's kindness and chose to order an evil deed.

God saw what Joash had done. He had turned away from the true God to worship useless idols. He had rejected God's message which Zechariah had given. He had forgotten the kindness of Jehoiada. He had killed God's messenger.

The Syrian army came against the people of Judah. God did not help Judah because of the people's sins, so they were defeated. The Syrians killed the leaders and severely wounded the king. As he lay wounded, his own servants killed Joash because of the killing of Zechariah.

## READ: 2 CHRONICLES 24
## QUESTIONS:
1. Why was there a great change in Joash's life? (2 Chronicles 24:15-18)
2. What message did Zechariah give to the people of Judah? (2 Chronicles 24:20)
3. Why were the Israelites defeated by a small army? (2 Chronicles 24:24)

# UZZIAH: THE KING WHO CHOSE TO ACT LIKE A PRIEST

Uzziah was only sixteen years old when he became king and he was king for fifty-two years. He set out to do right, and God helped him. He had victories over the enemies of Israel and became famous because of the strength God gave him. He built towers for defence and made sure that the army was well supplied with armour and weapons.

We read so many good things about King Uzziah, that it is sad to find that he became proud. Instead of thanking God for making him a strong king, he decided to act as if he was a priest as well as a king.

The temple at Jerusalem had courtyards where the people could go, but only the priests were allowed to enter the temple building. The priests were the descendants of Moses' brother, Aaron, and God had chosen them for the task. No one else could choose to be a priest. The temple, like the tabernacle before it, was meant to teach how sinful people could come to a holy God.

Everything that was done in the temple, was according to God's instructions.

Every day, morning and evening, the priests in the temple offered sacrifices for the sins of the people. They also burnt incense on the altar of incense every morning and evening. One day, King Uzziah decided that he would go into the temple to burn incense at the altar.

The priests saw the king enter the temple and they followed him. It was not easy to tell a king that he was wrong, but the priests did so. Uzziah was angry, but at that moment he was struck with leprosy. The priests could see the leprosy appearing on the king's forehead. They pushed him out of the temple, but Uzziah had realised that God was displeased with him, so he was ready to leave of his own accord.

King Uzziah, who had begun his reign so well, was a leper for the rest of his life. His son Jotham carried out the king's duties, because people with leprosy were not allowed to mix with others. The true story of King Uzziah reminds us that it is a very serious thing to choose to disobey God.

## READ: EXODUS 29:43-45; 30:7-8; 2 CHRONICLES 26
## QUESTIONS:

1. What was it that made Uzziah a strong and successful king? (2 Chronicles 26:4-5)
2. How did the king react, when the priests told him he was doing wrong? (2 Chronicles 26:18-19)
3. Who decided what should be done in the tabernacle (and later in the temple) and who said who should be consecrated (set apart by God) for the work? (Exodus 29:43-45; 30:7-8)

# EBED-MELECH WHO CHOSE TO STAND UP FOR GOD'S PROPHET

The prophet, Jeremiah, was chosen by God to speak His words to the people of Judah. The people did not like the message that Jeremiah brought, that God was going to punish them for their sinful ways. They were worshipping the false gods of the nations around them. God had warned them many times that if they did this, they would be taken away from the land He had given them.

Jeremiah had to tell the people that the disaster that they had been warned about since the time of Moses, was going to happen. They would be taken as captives to the land of Babylon. No one wanted to hear what Jeremiah said. The people liked listening to the false prophets who always told them good things. Sometimes Jeremiah was put into prison to stop him bringing God's message to the people of Judah.

There came a day when Jeremiah was put into a dungeon. It was not a prison cell with a door, it was more like a pit that he was lowered into by

ropes. Jeremiah sank into the muddy floor of the dungeon. It was a place where a prisoner could be left to starve to death.

Ebed-Melech was one of the king's officers. He heard what had happened to Jeremiah and he decided that he must speak to King Zedekiah, before Jeremiah died of hunger. The king commanded Ebed-Melech to take men with him and lift Jeremiah out of the dungeon. Ebed-Melech did as the king said. He took men and he took ropes. But he knew that the ropes would be painful and so he also took some old ragged clothes. He called to Jeremiah to put the rags under his arms and then the ropes, and so Jeremiah was pulled out of that terrible place.

It must have taken courage for Ebed-Melech to speak to the king about Jeremiah. Jeremiah's work was not finished: God had more for him to do.

God did not forget Ebed-Melech. He sent Jeremiah a message especially for him. Ebed-Melech was to be told that at the time when Jerusalem was taken by the Babylonians, he would be safe, because he trusted in God. Ebed-Melech's brave actions were done because he had faith in God.

## READ: JEREMIAH 38:1-13; 39:1-18
## QUESTIONS:
1. What was the complaint against Jeremiah? (Jeremiah 38:1-4)
2. What was the only way in or out of the dungeon? (Jeremiah 38:6, 11-13)
3. Why did God say that Ebed-Melech would not be killed when Jerusalem was attacked? (Jeremiah 39:18)

# JONAH: THE RELUCTANT PROPHET'S CHOICE

God had a message for the people of Nineveh and he told Jonah to go and speak to the people there. Jonah did not want to take God's message to Nineveh. He chose to go in the opposite direction. This disobedience brought Jonah into great trouble. The ship he took from Joppa to Tarshish (in Spain), was almost destroyed by a dreadful storm. Even the sailors were afraid and decided that someone had brought this trouble on them.

Jonah told the sailors that he was "running away" from God. This made the sailors decide that Jonah was the cause of the storm. They asked him what they should do and he told them that they must throw him into the sea. They did not want to do this, but eventually they did and straight away the sea became calm. The sailors realised that Jonah's God was the true God.

Even though Jonah had chosen to disobey God, God did not leave him to drown. God

had prepared a great fish to swallow Jonah, and Jonah was inside the fish for three days and three nights. In that strange place, Jonah prayed. God caused the fish to deposit Jonah on dry land.

When God told Jonah a second time, to go to Nineveh, Jonah obeyed. When he told the people of Nineveh that God would overthrow their city because of their wickedness, they repented. Even the king told the people to call upon God and to give up their evil ways.

When the people repented, God forgave their sin and did not destroy them. Jonah was not pleased. The reason he had disobeyed God at first, was that he knew that God would forgive the people if they gave up their evil ways. But the people of Nineveh had been very wicked and very cruel. Jonah did not want them to be forgiven. God was patient with Jonah, teaching him that God had pity on those who had not learned the difference between doing right and doing wrong.

## READ: THE BOOK OF JONAH
## QUESTIONS:
1. Why did Jonah not want to go to Nineveh? (Jonah 4:2)
2. What effect did the calming of the storm have on the sailors? (Jonah 1:11-16)
3. What effect did Jonah's message from God, have on the people of Nineveh? (Jonah 3:4-9)

# DANIEL: THE YOUNG MAN'S CHOICE

Nebuchadnezzar, King of Babylon, wanted intelligent, good-looking young men from good families, to be brought to Babylon from the land of Judah. These young men, when trained, could be useful to him.

Among those who were selected was a young man named Daniel. He soon found himself a student in a strange land, learning a new language as well as other subjects. The training was to last three years and during that time the students would be given the best food and wine from the king.

Daniel decided that he would not eat the king's food. The Bible does not tell us the reason, but it may have been his concern that some of the food was against the laws that God had given to the Israelites. The other possible reason was that the food could have been offered to idols before it was served. Whatever the reason, it was Daniel's desire to be faithful to God that made him speak to the steward in charge of the young men. This man was afraid that the king would be displeased if Daniel and his three friends did not look as healthy as the other young men. Daniel asked for a trial period of ten days, with vegetables to eat and water to drink. This request was granted. At the end of the ten days, Daniel and his friends looked healthier than the other young men. The steward who was responsible for them, allowed them to continue the diet they had requested.

After their three years training, the young men were brought before King Nebuchadnezzar. Daniel and his three friends were chosen to serve the king himself, because of their wisdom and understanding.

Taken from his home to a strange land where the people worshipped idols, Daniel had made his choice to be faithful to God. He and his three friends became trusted advisers of the king of Babylon.

### READ: DANIEL 1; 2 CHRONICLES 36:14-21
### QUESTIONS:
1. How had the people of Judah treated the prophets God had sent to them? (2 Chronicles 36:15-16)

2. What did Daniel decide? (Daniel 1:8)
3. What was the result of the "trial diet"? (Daniel 1:15-16)
4. What did the king decide about Daniel and his three friends, at the end of the three years' training? (Daniel 1:19-20)

# THREE YOUNG MEN WHO CHOSE NOT TO BOW DOWN

Three of the young men taken from Jerusalem to Babylon by King Nebuchadnezzar's army, were Hananiah, Mishael and Azariah. In Babylon their names were changed to Shadrach, Meshach and Abednego. They had to study for three years: learn the Babylonian language as well as many other subjects, so that they could be useful to the king.

When the three years of study were over, Nebuchadnezzar was very pleased with Shadrach, Meshach and Abednego, and so they were given work to do in the palace. Some time after this, Nebuchadnezzar had a huge golden image made. The image was about twenty-seven metres high. A special ceremony was held to dedicate the image, and all the important people from all over the Babylonian Empire were gathered together.

A herald announced to the people that when they heard the music play, they must all bow down and worship Nebuchadnezzar's image. For anyone who refused to do this, there was a punishment –

to be thrown into a burning furnace. The music played and the people bowed down. But some of the Babylonians were watching carefully. They saw that there were three men who had not worshipped the image: Shadrach, Meshach and Abednego.

When Nebuchadnezzar was told, he was very angry, and the three were brought before him. They were to be given another opportunity to obey him, and if they did not, they would be thrown into the furnace. They told the king that their God was able to rescue them from the furnace. But even if He did not rescue them, they would not worship the golden image.

At Nebuchadnezzar's command, the furnace was heated even more, the three men were tied up and thrown into the fire. The heat was so fierce that the men who dealt with them were killed. Then the king saw something that amazed him. Instead of three men, he saw four men walking about in the furnace. He said that the fourth person looked like the Son of God.

Nebuchadnezzar called Shadrach, Meshach and Abednego to come out of the furnace. They came to him, completely unharmed, even their clothes were not affected by the fire.

### READ: DANIEL 3; EXODUS 20:4-6
### QUESTIONS:
1. Why did Shadrach, Meshach and Abednego refuse to worship the golden image? (Exodus 20:4-6)
2. What answer did the three men give to the king? (Daniel 3:17-18)
3. What condition were Shadrach, Meshach and Abednego in, when they came out of the fire? (Daniel 3:27)

# DANIEL: THE GOVERNOR'S CHOICE

After the fall of the Babylonian Empire to the Medes and Persians, the Persian King Darius ruled the empire. Daniel was trusted by Darius, as he had been by Nebuchadnezzar. He became one of the three most important men in the kingdom. The king thought of making Daniel the chief governor next to himself.

The other governors and leaders of the people began to plot against Daniel. They looked for a fault so that they could complain about him but found nothing. They knew that he was faithful to God and looked for some way to find fault in the way he obeyed God's law.

These men came to the king. They suggested a new law should be made. For thirty days, no one should make a request to any god or man, but only to the king. Anyone who disobeyed would be thrown into the lion's den. The king signed the new law. Maybe he felt proud at the idea of everyone bringing their requests and depending on him alone.

Daniel knew about the law. But he did as he had always done since he was a young man – he prayed to God three times a day. He did not try to hide what he was doing, but with his window open he knelt and prayed.

The men who had brought the new law to the king, came to him again. This time they reported that Daniel was breaking the law by praying to God three times a day. The king was very sorry. He must have realised that he had been tricked by men who were jealous of Daniel. He could not change the law that he had signed. Daniel was thrown into the den and the door was sealed with a stone.

The king could not sleep that night. He could not eat, he would not have music played to him. Early in the morning he called to Daniel and Daniel answered him. He explained to the king that God had sent an angel to prevent the lions harming him.

As a young man, Daniel made his choice to be faithful to God. Years later, holding a very important position in the Persian Empire, he kept to that choice even when it seemed to put his life in danger. How wonderfully God protected Daniel, and what an effect this had on King Darius, who realised that Daniel's God was the true and living God.

## READ: DANIEL 6
## QUESTIONS:
1. What were the jealous men not able to do? (Daniel 6:4)
2. What did Daniel continue to do, as he had done since he was young? (Daniel 6:10)
3. What effect did Daniel's safety in the lion's den have on King Darius? (Daniel 6:25-27)

## CHOICES IN THE BOOK OF ESTHER
# QUEEN VASHTI'S CHOICE

King Ahasuerus of Persia made a great feast for the important people of the land. Queen Vashti also made a feast for the women of the palace. On the seventh day of his feast, the king had been drinking wine. He sent a message to the queen, asking her to come to him wearing her royal crown. She was a beautiful woman and he wanted to let the people look at her.

It would have been expected that the king's wife would obey him. But Queen Vashti refused to come. She was not willing to be "shown off" to all the king's guests. King Ahasuerus was very angry. He sent for his advisors. What should be done to the queen who would not obey the king's command?

The king's advisors said that Vashti should no longer be queen. The king should find someone else to take her place. They said this because they were afraid that all their wives would follow Vashti's example and refuse to obey their husbands.

So it came about that Vashti was no longer a queen living in a palace. We do not know what happened to her because the Bible does not mention her name again. Was she right to choose to disobey her husband? The Bible says that wives should obey their husbands, but it never tells us to obey anyone who asks us to do something that is wrong. Probably the king would never have put his wife in such a situation if he had not been drinking too much wine.

### READ: ESTHER 1
### QUESTIONS:
1. Why did King Ahasuerus send for Queen Vashti? (Esther 1:10-11)
2. What did the king's advisors say should be done to Vashti? (Esther 1:19)
3. What were the king's advisors afraid of? (Esther 1:16-20)

# THE KING'S CHOICES AND THE CHOICE MORDECAI MADE

King Ahasuerus chose to follow the advice he was given. Vashti would no longer be queen. His advisors also suggested that many beautiful young women should be brought to him, so that he could choose a new queen.

The advisors did not tell him who should be the new queen. This would be his choice. From all the young women summoned to the palace, King Ahasuerus chose Esther. She belonged to a Jewish family, in exile in the land of Persia. Esther's parents had died and she had been looked after by her older cousin Mordecai. Mordecai looked after her as if she was his daughter.

After he had chosen a new queen, Ahasuerus made another choice. This was to appoint someone to the highest position in the land, second only to the king himself. He chose a man named Haman, a choice which would have very serious results in the days ahead.

Mordecai heard of a plot against the king's life and told Queen Esther. She informed the king and the conspirators were put to death. This showed Mordecai's loyalty to Ahasuerus and yet when Haman was promoted, Mordecai refused to bow down to him, as others did. The Bible does not tell us why Mordecai chose to act this way, but it may have been because he knew that Haman belonged to the enemies of the Jewish people – a people who God had said should be destroyed. Mordecai may also have seen that Haman was a proud man, who wanted the sort of worship that should only be given to God.

Mordecai's choice almost brought disaster to the Jewish nation. It also brought Haman's true character to light.

## READ: ESTHER 2; 3:1-2
## QUESTIONS:
1. What was the advice that King Ahasuerus chose to follow? (Esther 2:2-4)
2. What relation was Mordecai to Esther? (Esther 2:7)
3. Who did the king choose to be second only to the king himself? (Esther 3:1)
4. What did Mordecai choose not to do? (Esther 3:2)

# HAMAN'S CHOICE AND QUEEN ESTHER'S CHOICE

Haman was very angry because Mordecai refused to bow down to him. In his powerful position, he could have punished Mordecai, but this was not enough for him. He decided to destroy all the Jews throughout the Persian Empire. To do this, he first spoke to the king. He persuaded the king that there were certain people throughout the empire who did not obey the king's laws. He gained permission to see to it that these people were destroyed. A date was set and letters were sent out which stated that all Jews, young and old, were to be killed on that particular day. Haman also decided that he would be responsible for Mordecai's death. He set up a gallows about twenty-three metres high, to hang him.

Esther was troubled about Mordecai. Her maids told her that he was sitting outside the king's gate, clothed in sackcloth instead of his usual clothing. She sent out clothes to him, but he would not take them. She then sent someone to

# KING AHASUERUS MAKES SOME MORE CHOICES

As he sat on his royal throne, the king saw Esther waiting. He held out the golden sceptre. He chose to let her come and make her request. Esther had to be careful. Haman was the king's favourite. She would not hurry to speak about her people. She simply invited the king to bring Haman to the banquet she had prepared.

She repeated this for a second day and only then began to plead that her people the Jews, should not be destroyed. When the king wanted to know who would dare to destroy the queen's own people, the Jews, Esther had to name Haman.

The king was very angry. Only the night before, the king had learned about Mordecai saving his life. He knew from this that the Jews were not at all as Haman had described them. He realised he had been deceived and gave orders for Haman to be hanged on the gallows he had prepared for Mordecai. He had chosen to believe Esther and he then promoted Mordecai to the important position that Haman had held.

## READ: ESTHER 5-7
## QUESTIONS:

1. Did Esther hurry to make her request to the king, if not, how did she go about it? (Esther 5:3-8)
2. How did the king react to hearing how Haman had deceived him? (Esther 7:4-7)
3. What was the end of all Haman's plotting? (Esther 7:10)

# EXTRA: GOD'S PROVIDENCE

God's providence is the way God rules over everything and cares for His people. The Book of Esther does not mention God, but the events were certainly brought about by God's providential care for the Jewish people. Examples are:

1. Esther became queen when someone would be needed to plead for the Jews.
2. The king could not sleep, he had the record book read to him. That was how he learned that Mordecai had saved his life. He learned this first at the time Haman was planning to kill Mordecai, and when Esther was determined to plead for her people. Haman had planned to destroy the Jewish nation. But long before, God had promised Abraham that the Saviour would be born from his descendants.

The Book of Esther shows us how wrong choices people make, can never prevent God keeping His promises.

**READ: ESTHER 8–10**

# NEHEMIAH: THE CUPBEARER'S CHOICE

The King of Babylon took people from the land of Judah to Babylon. God had warned the people that this would happen if they disobeyed Him and worshipped idols like the nations around them. In time, the Babylonian Empire was conquered by the Persians. Nehemiah was among the Jews who were living in Persia. He was cupbearer to King Artaxerxes, which means that he looked after the king's wine.

One day, Nehemiah had a visit from his brother Hanani and some other Jewish people. Nehemiah asked about the situation in Jerusalem. He was very sad when he heard that the city wall was broken down and the gates had been burned. Over the weeks that followed this news, he spent time praying. He asked God to remember His promise, that when His people were sorry for their evil ways and obeyed His commands, He would bring them back to their own land. Nehemiah also asked God to help him when he was with the king.

One day, a few months after the news from Jerusalem, Nehemiah served wine to the king. The king noticed that Nehemiah looked sad and asked him why this was. Nehemiah could have hidden his sadness from the king and no doubt this was what the king's servants would be expected to do. But after all his praying, he must have felt sure that God wanted him to do something about the situation in Jerusalem.

Nehemiah explained his sadness and the king allowed him to make a request. The result was that he was allowed to go to Jerusalem for a time, with letters from the king to make sure he had a safe journey and the materials he needed. Nehemiah chose to work as well as pray for the good of Jerusalem. But in his choice he was guided by God. He was God's chosen man for the work.

Nehemiah did travel to Jerusalem. He did organise the people to rebuild the city wall, even though the enemies of the Jews tried to stop him. Nehemiah had trusted God to help him to speak to the king. He then trusted God to protect those who worked to rebuild the wall.

## READ: NEHEMIAH 1; 2:1-8; 4:7-14
## QUESTIONS:
1. Why was Nehemiah sad about news from Jerusalem? (Nehemiah 1:2-3)
2. What was the first thing he did about the situation? (Nehemiah 1:4-11; 2:4)
3. What three things did Nehemiah do when the workers were threatened? (Nehemiah 4:7, 13-14)

# THE KING WHO CHOSE TO DESTROY LITTLE CHILDREN

The true story of the visit of the wise men to Jerusalem after Jesus was born, is well known. King Herod was very troubled when the wise men arrived. He obviously knew that a special birth had been foretold in Old Testament days. When he inquired, the priests and scribes were actually able to tell him the birthplace of the promised one. This had been written about by the prophet Micah (Micah 5:2) about 700 years before.

Herod told the wise men to go to Bethlehem and look for the child there. He also told them to report back to him where the child was to be found, so that he could go to worship Him as well.

Herod had no intention of worshipping the promised King. He had set his mind on destroying Him. God knows our thoughts and intentions and He knew what was in the mind of King Herod. God used a dream to send a message to the wise men, that they should not go back to King Herod. The wise men obeyed and went back to their own country a different way.

Mary, the mother of Jesus, was married to Joseph. Joseph also received a message from God. In a dream, an angel appeared to him, telling him to take Mary and the child, Jesus, into Egypt. Joseph did as the angel had told him and they remained in Egypt until God told Joseph that it was safe to return to Israel.

Time went by in Jerusalem, and King Herod became angry as he realised that the wise men were not coming back as he had told them to. He made a cruel and terrible choice. He ordered that all the little boys up to two years old, in and around Bethlehem, should be put to death. How cruel, to kill defenceless children and bring sorrow into many homes. Long ago, the prophet Jeremiah had spoken of a time when mothers would weep for the children they had lost.

No one, not even the king, could defeat God's purposes. The Lord Jesus was protected from harm, until the time came when He willingly gave His life on the cross, a perfect sacrifice for sinners like us.

## READ: JEREMIAH 31:15; MATTHEW 2; MICAH 5:2
## QUESTIONS:

1. How was Herod able to tell the wise men the place where the Lord Jesus would be born? (Matthew 2:4-6; Micah 5:2)
2. What two warnings did God give? (Matthew 2:12-13)
3. Matthew 2:18 is taken from Jeremiah's prophecy (Jeremiah 31:15). Rachel was Jacob's wife at the time of the beginning of the nation of Israel. What was "Rachel weeping for her children" a picture of? Who was weeping in the days of King Herod?

# THE PHARISEES: THE RELIGIOUS LEADERS' CHOICE

All through the Old Testament days, God sent prophets to bring His message to His people. The prophets spoke of One whom God would send to be the Saviour of all who trust in Him. They also spoke of someone who would prepare the way for the promised Saviour (Isaiah 40:3; Malachi 4:5). Malachi was the last of the Old Testament prophets, and about four hundred years after his prophecy, a man named John began calling on the people to repent. Many people came to John. They confessed their sins and were baptized by him in the River Jordan. John became known as "John the Baptist".

The Pharisees were a group of religious leaders in the land of Israel. They were proud of keeping all God's commandments and even added rules of their own. They did not realise that their hearts were sinful and so they did not go to John for baptizm. Water could not wash away sin, but being baptized by John was a sign of being sorry for sin and wanting to change.

The Pharisees chose not to be baptized. They did not understand how sinful their pride was. They did not see that what mattered to them was to appear good, but that this was not pleasing to God. When the Lord Jesus began to go about teaching the people and healing the sick, the Pharisees refused to accept that he had come from God. The Lord Jesus spoke some of His sternest words to the Pharisees and other religious leaders. He said that they were hypocrites – acting a part. Just as the Pharisees had chosen not to believe John the Baptist's teaching, they also chose not to believe in the Lord Jesus. They heard Him and wanted Him to be put to death.

There are still people who are very religious, but whose hearts are full of sinful pride. They think that God is pleased with them because they "go to church" and maybe give money to charity. We need to be sure that God has forgiven our sins because we are trusting in the Lord Jesus Christ. Our faith must be in His perfect life and His death on the cross, not in our own "goodness".

## READ: MATTHEW 3:1-9; MATTHEW 23:13-14; 23-28; LUKE 7:29-30
## QUESTIONS:
1. Why did the Pharisees choose not to be baptized? (What was it that John told the people to do, which the Pharisees thought they did not need to do? (Matthew 3:1-2)
2. What was wrong with the prayers of the Pharisees? (Matthew 23:14)
3. What had the Pharisees neglected? (Matthew 23:23)

# NICODEMUS: THE PHARISEE WHO CHOSE TO MEET JESUS

Nicodemus was a Pharisee and a teacher of God's law. But he was honest enough to know that no one could do the things Jesus did, unless He had come from God. He decided to meet the Lord Jesus, and he came to see Him at night. This may have been because he did not want others to know about his meeting with Jesus. There was also a practical reason. It could be difficult to talk with Jesus in the daytime, when people crowded around Him.

The Lord Jesus told Nicodemus that he needed to be "born again". Nicodemus did not understand this. He was a religious man, but he did not understand that only God's Holy Spirit could give him new life. He thought he could please God by keeping God's law, but he needed to know that he was a sinner who needed God's forgiveness.

Meeting the Lord Jesus and listening to Him must have started a change in Nicodemus' life. The next time we read about him, he spoke out about Jesus to other Pharisees. He told them that it was unfair to pass judgement on Jesus without hearing what He said or seeing what He was doing.

The Bible tells us one thing more about Nicodemus. When the Lord Jesus was crucified, even His disciples were afraid. Peter, who really loved the Lord Jesus, actually said that he did not know Him. Seeing the terrible way Jesus was treated, must have made the disciples fear what might happen to them.

However, two men who had not been known as friends of Jesus, came forward to care for His body after He had been crucified. One was a wealthy man named Joseph. He asked permission to take the body from the cross. Then Nicodemus came with the spices that Jews used to prepare a body for burial. They did everything that was necessary and then laid the body of Jesus in a tomb.

## READ: JOHN 3:1-21; JOHN 7:45-53; JOHN 19:38-42
## QUESTIONS:

1. Why did Nicodemus choose to meet Jesus? (John 3:2)
2. In what way did Nicodemus stand up to the other Pharisees? (John 7:51)
3. How did Nicodemus show his love for the Lord Jesus, at a time when even the disciples were afraid? (John 19:39-42)

# THE FOUR FRIENDS: A DETERMINED CHOICE

If you had a friend who was ill for a long time, I expect you would want to help them in any way you could. Of course, nowadays we have lots of medicines which the doctor will use to help us to get well.

At the time the Lord Jesus was here on earth, there were not so many medicines and seeing a doctor probably cost a lot of money. Four men had a friend who was paralysed – he could not move. Out of all the ways they could help their friend, they chose to take him to the Lord Jesus. The man could not walk, so his friends carried him on his bed (a bed at that time was usually a sleeping mat).

The house where the Lord Jesus was speaking to the people, was in Capernaum. It was so full, that the four men could not get their friend to Jesus. But these men were very determined. The house would have had a flat roof. The men moved some of the roof tiles and let their friend down to where Jesus was.

Jesus saw that these men had faith: they had brought their friend to Him because they really believed that He could heal him. He told the paralysed man that his sins were forgiven. To have our sins forgiven is more important than being healed. Only God can forgive us because it is His law that we have broken. Jesus then told the man to get up, pick up his bed, and go home. He did exactly as Jesus told him – he was no longer paralysed. How wonderful that the choice his friends made, resulted in him being made well. We may have friends who need to hear about the Lord Jesus. They may not need to have their bodies healed, but they do need to have their sins forgiven. We can tell them that Jesus is our Friend, because our sin, which separated us from Him, has all been forgiven.

## READ: MARK 2:1-12
## QUESTIONS:

1. How do we know the four friends were determined that the paralysed man should come to where Jesus was? (Mark 2:4)
2. What were the first two things that Jesus said to the sick man? (Mark 2: 5, 11)
3. Think of some ways that you can help your friends to learn about the Lord Jesus.

# JOHN THE BAPTIST'S BRAVE CHOICE

The King of Israel, when Jesus was born, was known as Herod the Great. After his death, members of his family reigned over different parts of the land. (Of course the Roman Emperor held the real power, but nations governed by Rome were allowed to have their own "king".) The King Herod we read about in Matthew Chapter 14 would have been one of Herod the Great's sons, Antipas.

This King Herod had a brother who married a woman named Herodias. He then did something that God's law forbade. He took Herodias as his own wife. John the Baptist knew what the king had done and he knew that it was wrong. Bravely, he confronted the king with his sinful action.

Herod would have liked to have put John to death. However, he was afraid of the effect this would have on the people, because they believed that John was a prophet sent to them by God, so he had John put into prison.

Herodias had a daughter named Salome. Part of King Herod's birthday celebrations one year, was having Salome dance for him and his guests. The king was so delighted with this, that he promised to give Salome whatever she asked. It seems that she turned to her mother with the question, "what should I ask?" Herodias told her daughter to ask for the head of John the Baptist.

King Herod had made a promise in front of his guests, so he gave the order for John to be beheaded. This was done, and so Herodias had her revenge for what John had said.

John the Baptist had been faithful in carrying out the task God had given him. He knew that his work had been to prepare the people of Israel for the coming of the promised Messiah. Many people had come to John to be baptized, showing that they had repented of their sins. He pointed the people to the Lord Jesus, the promised Saviour. How terrible that his life was taken, because he had been brave enough to speak honestly to the king. But for John, as for all who trust in the Lord Jesus, death was the entrance into a wonderful life, where there is no sin, sorrow or pain.

### READ: MATTHEW 14:1-12; JOHN 1:19-34
### QUESTIONS:
1. How did John the Baptist know that Jesus was the Son of God? (John 1:32-34)
2. Why did King Herod want to put John to death? (Matthew 14:3-4)
3. Why did Salome make her terrible request? (Matthew 14:7-8)

# THE MAN WHO CHOSE TO SPEAK THE TRUTH

One day Jesus passed a man who had been blind from the day he was born. Think of a little child who never saw the face of his mother or father. Think of his parents' sadness as they realised what was wrong. Now an adult, he had no way to make a living, except to sit at the roadside and beg from passers-by.

Instead of walking on, Jesus stayed by the blind man and made clay which He put on the man's eyes. He told the man to wash at a pool known as the Pool of Siloam. The man did as Jesus had told him and came back able to see. People who had seen him before began to question whether this really could be the same man. When they had questioned the man about what had happened to him, they took him to the Pharisees.

The man had been healed on the Sabbath day, the day when God had said people should rest from their work. When the Pharisees heard what had happened, they began to argue about whether Jesus could have come from God, because he had not kept the Sabbath day. They then began to question the man about how he had received his sight.

People were afraid to say that they believed that Jesus had come from God, because if they did so, they could be banned from attending the synagogue. It would be a great disgrace to be "put out" of the synagogue where the Jewish people met to hear teaching from the Old Testament. But the man who had been given his sight, chose to speak the truth about the Lord Jesus. He rightly said that only someone who had come from God could do such a wonderful miracle. The Pharisees told the man that he was banned from going to the synagogue. They would have been quite happy if the once blind man had just thanked God for his sight. But they so hated the Lord Jesus, that they could not bear to hear of anyone who believed in Him.

Later, Jesus came and spoke to the man. He made it clear to him that the One who had restored his sight was the Son of God. The man believed. He saw what the Pharisees refused to see.

## READ: MATTHEW 12:9-12; JOHN 9
## QUESTIONS:
1. How did Jesus explain that it was not wrong to heal on the Sabbath day? (Matthew 12:11-12)
2. Why did the man's parents not want to answer questions about him? (John 9:19-22)
3. What did the blind man understand about the Lord Jesus? (John 9:30-33)

# TWO SISTERS: TWO CHOICES

The leaders of the Jewish people were jealous of the Lord Jesus. They did not like to see the people listening to Him instead of to them. They did not like to see the miracles of healing that He did which made many people come to Him. They did not welcome His coming into the world.

There were two sisters who did welcome the Lord Jesus into their home. They lived in a village called Bethany, a few miles from Jerusalem. One day, when Jesus was with them, Martha was busy preparing a meal. Her sister Mary was sitting listening to Jesus. Martha became very upset because her sister was not helping her. She spoke to the Lord Jesus about it and wanted Him to ask Mary to help her.

The Lord Jesus spoke gently to Martha because He saw how anxious and upset she was. But He would not ask Mary to help her, because He said that Mary's choice was good. Mary had chosen to listen to Jesus. This was more important than an elaborate meal.

Mary and Martha both loved the Lord Jesus. Maybe Martha chose to show her love by making an especially good meal. A simple meal, with more time listening to Jesus, would have been better.

We can learn from these two sisters about the choices we make. We have to think about what is really important. The most important thing of all is to welcome the Lord Jesus into our lives, as Mary and Martha welcomed Him into their home. We do this when we ask Him to forgive our sin and then guide us in all that we do. We will then want to set aside time each day to read from the Bible and pray. We will also want to meet with others who love the Lord Jesus, on Sundays and at other times. There are many things that are not wrong, but that can crowd out our time of prayer and reading. We need to remember Mary's choice, and the importance of time learning from the Bible and speaking to God in prayer.

**READ: PSALM 119:105; PROVERBS 3:5-6; LUKE 10:38-42**
**QUESTIONS:**
1. Why was Martha upset? (Luke 10:40)
2. What did the Lord Jesus say about Mary's choice? (Luke 10:42)
3. How can we be sure that God will guide us? (Proverbs 3:5-6)

# THE TEN LEPERS: DIFFERENT CHOICES

Leprosy is a disease that can be treated now. In Bible times, there was no medicine to make a leper better. Anyone with leprosy had to live apart from other people, so it was a very sad day when any person found that they had this disease.

One day ten lepers called to the Lord Jesus from a distance. They did not dare come near to Him. They asked Him to have mercy on them. Jesus simply told them to show themselves to the priests. It was a duty of the priests to inspect a leper and say whether the disease had been cured or not. As the lepers set off to see the priest, their illness was cured.

All the ten men had made a choice as to what they should do. They all called to Jesus for help. One leper, realising that he was better, chose to go back to the Lord Jesus, to thank Him. He was a Samaritan. The Samaritans were people who had been brought into the land of Israel many years before. They did not belong to the Jewish people. Jews and Samaritans usually had nothing to do with each other. But this Samaritan was the only one who took the trouble to say thank you to the Lord Jesus. The other nine lepers chose to go on their way with no giving of thanks.

The Lord Jesus asked where the other nine men who had been healed were. He spoke kindly to the one who had thanked Him, and had praised God for his healing, "Your faith has made you well." Faith had brought him to the only one who could heal him.

God has given us life and a beautiful world to live in. Do we thank Him, or are we like the ungrateful nine lepers?

### READ: LEVITICUS 13:46; LEVITICUS 14:2; LUKE 17:11-19
### QUESTIONS:
1. Why do we read in Luke 17:12 that the ten men did not come close to where Jesus was? (Leviticus 13:46)
2. Why did Jesus tell them to go to the priests? (Luke 17:14 and Leviticus 14:2)
3. How many were healed? How many gave thanks? (Luke 17:14-15)

# THE RICH YOUNG MAN'S CHOICE

A young man hurried to see the Lord Jesus. He had an important question to ask. What must he do so that he could have eternal life? Jesus reminded him of God's commands to respect life, marriage, property, truthfulness and our parents. The young man assured Him that he had always obeyed these commandments.

The Lord Jesus knows our hearts. He knew what this young man lacked. He told him that he should sell his possessions and give the money to the poor. Then he should follow Jesus.

This young man was rich. He thought of his many possessions and he walked away feeling very sad. The Lord Jesus had seen that the things he owned meant too much to him. He was not willing to put God first in his life. If he had done what Jesus told him, he would have had "treasure in heaven", which would have been his forever.

One day, when the Lord Jesus was teaching the people, he had said that our treasures on earth do not last. They may be attacked by moths or by rust, or they may be stolen. Giving to God all that He has given to us, will give us treasure in heaven, which lasts for ever. The choice that the rich young man made, showed that he loved his possessions more than he loved God. Although he could say that he kept the second part of the ten commandments, he had not kept the first part, which is all about our love and obedience to God: the way we worship Him, the way we use His name and the way we use His day.

If we love the Lord Jesus, He will have first place in our lives. When we love other things more than Him, it is like having an idol, a false god. There are many things that are not wrong, but can take over our lives so that we forget about needing to grow into strong Christians. If prayer and Bible reading are neglected, we will not grow in our love for the Lord Jesus and our desire to serve Him. It will help us if we remember the true story of the rich young man.

**READ: EXODUS 20:1-17; MATTHEW 6:19-21; MARK 10:17-22**

**QUESTIONS:**

1. How many of the ten commandments are about our love for God and how many are about our love for other people? (Exodus 20:1-17)
2. What can happen to the things we treasure in this world? (Matthew 6:19)
3. What did the rich young man love more than God? (Mark 10:21-22)

# ZACCHAEUS: WHO CHOSE TO DO RIGHT

Tax collectors in New Testament days were not popular. They cheated, taking more money than necessary so they could keep some for themselves. Zacchaeus was no exception. He was a rich tax collector at Jericho.

When Jesus was in Jericho, Zacchaeus set out to see Him. Being short he could not see Jesus in the crowd so climbed a tree to get a better view. What a surprise when Jesus called him by name to hurry down. The Lord Jesus had chosen Zacchaeus' house to visit that day.

Zacchaeus was filled with joy. Tax collectors were usually despised by the people, so he gladly received this guest. Of course, the crowd grumbled that Jesus was going to the house of such a sinful person.

That day a great change happened in Zacchaeus' life. Jesus spoke to him and Zacchaeus chose to give half of his possessions to the poor. Anything he had taken wrongly, he would pay back four times as much.

Zacchaeus shows us the change that takes place when someone trusts in the Lord Jesus. The person's whole outlook is changed. They want to please God instead of selfishly pleasing themselves. Zacchaeus showed that he knew he had done wrong. How different from the Pharisees who saw no need of forgiveness for their pride and hypocrisy.

God freely forgives those who confess their sin, but those who refuse to seek God's forgiveness will one day face the punishment their sins deserve. How wonderful to know that the Lord Jesus has taken sin's punishment for everyone who trusts in Him.

### READ: LUKE 19:1-10; 2 CORINTHIANS 5:17
### QUESTIONS:
1. How did Zacchaeus show that a real change had taken place in his life? (Luke 19:8)
2. Put 2 Corinthians 5:17 into your own words. How does this apply to Zacchaeus?
3. What does Luke 19:10 tell us about why the Lord Jesus met with Zacchaeus?

# A WIDOW'S CHOICE TO GIVE EVERYTHING

In the women's courtyard of the temple at Jerusalem, there were chests where people could put money. These chests were called the treasury. The money was used for the work of the temple and all the things that were needed there.

One day, when the Lord Jesus had been speaking to the people in the temple, He saw some rich people putting money into the treasury. Some might let their coins make a lot of noise as they dropped them into the chest. Others would hear a lot of money being given, and they would think how generous the rich person was. As Jesus watched, a poor widow came along. Life was very difficult for a woman with no husband to support her. She could not give a lot of money. All she had was two of the smallest copper coins then in use. She put them both into the treasury. She had nothing left for herself.

It is not likely that this poor woman wanted anyone to see what she was giving. Her two little coins would have dropped quietly into the chest. But someone had seen and understood what she had done. The Lord Jesus said that this woman had given more than the rich people. They all had plenty left for themselves! She had given all that she had.

We sometimes hear of rich people giving large sums of money to charity. We might feel that we have so little to give to help others. It is good to know that God understands when our "little" is given out of love for Him.

In Old Testament days, people were taught to give one tenth of their money to God's work. The New Testament teaches that we should give in proportion to what God has given to us (1 Corinthians 16:2).

We cannot put our money into the temple treasury that we have been reading about. How do we give? If we are Christians, we will want to be part of a local church and give to support its work. Missionaries who go to other countries to tell people about the Lord Jesus, need support from those who remain at home. In the United Kingdom there are also many works that need support, such as prison ministries, open air preaching, beach missions in the summer.

We are not to give because we feel we have to, but because we love the Lord Jesus who gave His life for us.

### READ: 1 SAMUEL 16:7; LUKE 21:1-4; 2 CORINTHIANS 9:7
### QUESTIONS:
1. What is the difference between how we look at people and how God looks? (1 Samuel 16:7)
2. What was special about the poor widow's gift? (Luke 21:3-4)
3. If we give to help others, should we do this just because we feel it is our duty? (2 Corinthians 9:7)

# THE CENTURION WHO CHOSE TO BELIEVE

In New Testament days, Israel was part of the Roman Empire and Roman soldiers were present in the land, to keep order. In Matthew's Gospel we read about a Roman officer, a centurion. His servant was very ill. He must have heard about the wonderful miracles that the Lord Jesus had done, and so he came to seek His help.

Jesus was willing to go with the centurion to heal his servant. But although he was a Roman officer, he was not a proud man. He told Jesus that he was not worthy of having Him come to his house. He then showed his faith by saying that he knew that Jesus could heal by a word, without seeing or touching the sick man. The centurion knew that his soldiers obeyed his word. He believed that the Lord Jesus had such power over disease, that a word from Him would bring healing.

Jesus told the people who were with Him that He had not seen faith like the centurion's in all the land of Israel. He told the centurion that he could go. He had believed and what he asked would be done. The servant was healed as Jesus spoke.

Many of the Jewish people did not believe that Jesus was the Son of God, the promised Saviour, even though they had all of the Old Testament to help them. But here was a Roman soldier who understood more than they did. He chose to believe in the power of the Lord Jesus to heal. He knew that Jesus was not an ordinary man.

The Bible teaches us that God gives us faith to believe that Jesus can be our Saviour (Ephesians 2:8). When the Holy Spirit helps us to understand that we are sinners who need a Saviour, we should ask God to give us faith. Faith in the Lord Jesus is more than just believing that He can save people from their sinfulness. It means that I believe that if I trust in Him, He will save me.

## READ: MATTHEW 8:5-13
## QUESTIONS:
1. Why did the centurion ask the Lord Jesus not to come to his house? (Matthew 8:8)
2. What did he believe that Jesus was able to do? (Matthew 8:8)
3. What did Jesus say about the centurion's faith? (Matthew 8:10)

# A WOMAN'S TWO CHOICES: WHEN SICK AND WHEN HEALED

Jesus met a woman who had been ill for twelve years. She had been seen by many doctors, but instead of getting better, she got worse. She had spent all her money on trying to get well. Then she heard about the Lord Jesus. He had healed many people from all sorts of illnesses.

The illness she had, meant that she was treated as "unclean". She could not have normal contact with other people. It would be difficult for her to meet Jesus, but she made a plan. She would make her way through the crowd around Him, until she was right behind Him. She would not draw attention to herself. She would simply get close enough to touch the hem of His clothing. Surely, as He had such power, some of that power might come to her, even without her being seen by Him.

She carried out her plan. Passing through the crowd until she stood behind Jesus and then putting out her hand to touch the hem of His garment. Something wonderful happened. The woman knew straight away that she was better.

Then she heard the Lord Jesus ask His disciples who had touched His clothes. The disciples were amazed that He asked such a question, while people were pressing all around Him. But Jesus knew that He had been touched by someone who needed His healing power.

What should the woman do? She knew that she had been healed. Must she speak to Jesus, in front of so many people? She made her choice. Trembling, she moved to where Jesus could see her and she knelt before Him. She told Him all about what she had done. He spoke kindly to her and told her that her faith had made her well. It was faith that brought this very sick woman to Jesus. She had believed that He could heal her.

## READ: MARK 5:25-34
## QUESTIONS:

1. How long had the woman we read about in these verses, been ill and why was she now poor as well as ill? (Mark 5:25-26)
2. What was the question that surprised the disciples? (Mark 5:30-32)
3. Who did the sick woman have faith in and what was the result of her faith?

# MARY'S LOVING CHOICE

Mary had something precious. It was a pound (about 450 grams) of fragrant oil called spikenard. Mary used all this fragrant oil one day when Jesus was visiting Bethany.

Mary and Martha had a brother named Lazarus who had been very ill. His sisters had sent a message to the Lord Jesus. Jesus did not go straight away to Bethany, and when He did arrive there, Lazarus had died a few days before. Mary and Martha's sadness turned to joy and thankfulness when Jesus restored Lazarus to life. So when Jesus again came to Bethany, the sisters had an added reason to welcome and show their love for this special guest.

It was a wonderful occasion, with Lazarus able to enjoy a meal with his sisters and the Lord Jesus and His disciples. Martha was serving the meal. What could Mary do to show her love for the Lord? She took her precious spikenard oil and poured it over Jesus' feet. Of course, in that country, water was usually provided to wash the feet of visitors who had walked along the dusty roads. This was not enough for Mary, and the house was soon filled with the lovely perfume, from her fragrant oil.

Judas Iscariot, one of the twelve disciples, complained about what Mary had done. He said that the oil could have been sold and the money given to the poor. But Judas did not really care about the poor. In fact, he stole some of the money that he was supposed to look after for the disciples.

The Lord Jesus understood Mary's loving action. He knew that this was the way she had chosen to show her love. He reproved Judas for his critical words. He knew that Judas was not honest and that unlike Mary, he had no love for the Lord Jesus.

We cannot do what Mary did, but we can show our love for Jesus by doing the things the Bible teaches us to do. We can show kindness to others, especially Christians who need our help, either those we know or those in other lands who are going through difficult days.

## READ: JOHN 12:1-8; JOHN 14:15; GALATIANS 6:10
## QUESTIONS:
1. Did the Lord Jesus reprove Mary for using all her precious oil? (John 12:7-8)
2. How can we show our love for the Lord Jesus? (John 14:15)
3. Who should we show kindness to? (Galatians 6:10)

# JUDAS: A TERRIBLE CHOICE

Judas Iscariot was one of the twelve disciples of the Lord Jesus. He saw all the miracles that Jesus did and heard all His teaching. Like the other disciples he was sent for a time to preach the Gospel and heal the sick. But all was not well with Judas. We read in John 12:6 that he was a thief. He was supposed to look after the disciples' money, but he helped himself to what he wanted.

The priests and other religious leaders of the Jews, wanted to put the Lord Jesus to death. They hated Him because the people listened to Him instead of them. They saw that the miracles He did were real, but they never gave thanks that sick people were made well or blind people given their sight again. We would say that they were jealous.

Judas knew about the plans of the religious leaders. The dreadful choice that he made, was to offer to help them. The leaders were afraid of the people's reaction if they arrested Jesus in public. Judas could help them to find Him when there were no crowds around Him.

Judas went to see the chief priests. They were pleased that he had come to them and promised him money if he helped them.

The Lord Jesus met with His disciples to eat the Passover meal with them. During the meal He warned them that He would be betrayed (handed over to His enemies) and He knew who His betrayer was. Judas left during the meal but the disciples did not know why. After He had talked with them, Jesus took His eleven disciples to a quiet place – the Garden of Gethsemane.

The priests had provided Judas with soldiers. He led them to the garden and greeted the Lord Jesus so that the soldiers would not make any mistake in the darkness. The soldiers arrested Jesus and took Him to the High Priest. The Lord Jesus was not given a fair trial. He was sentenced to death.

When Judas knew that Jesus had been condemned, he was sorry for what he had done. But he did not truly repent and seek God's forgiveness, instead he took his own life by hanging himself.

This true story of Judas reminds us that it is possible to know a lot about the Lord Jesus and to spend time with Christian people, without true faith. Judas' heart had not been changed and the choice he made to betray Jesus was surely the most terrible of all the choices we read about in the Bible.

### READ: JOHN 12:1-6; MATTHEW 26:14-16; 47-50; MATTHEW 27:1-5
### QUESTIONS:
1. What do we learn about Judas from John 12:1-6?
2. What did Judas receive for promising to betray Jesus to those who hated Him? (Matthew 26:15) and what happened to this money? (Matthew 27:3-5)
3. What sign did Judas give to the soldiers, so that they would know who to arrest? (Matthew 26:48-49)

# PILATE: WHO CHOSE TO PLEASE THE PEOPLE

Pontius Pilate was the governor of Judea, the southern part of the land of Israel. He was in charge of the Roman soldiers there and he also had power to pass the death sentence on offenders. The Jewish leaders put the Lord Jesus on trial. They decided that He should be put to death for claiming to be the Son of God. They were not allowed to carry out the death sentence and so had to take Jesus to Pilate, the Roman Governor.

Pilate listened to all the accusations the Jews brought against Jesus. He knew that their real reason for wanting Him put to death was envy. They could not deny that the Lord Jesus had done many miracles and that crowds of people had followed Him and listened to His teaching. It was Passover time in Jerusalem. The Passover feast was held every year, reminding the people of how God had brought the Israelites out of Egypt, many years before. At the time of the feast, Pilate would release one prisoner, as the people requested. On this occasion, he suggested that Jesus should be released. The Jewish leaders persuaded the people to ask for Barabbas to be freed. Barabbas was accused of murder.

Pilate had to make a choice. He had found no fault in the Lord Jesus. He found Him "not guilty" of any of the charges brought against Him. But Pilate did not want trouble in Judea. The Roman government would not be pleased if he did not control the people.

Pilate deliberately washed his hands in front of the people. This was his way of saying that he would not be guilty of putting an innocent person to death. He handed Jesus over to the Jews and released Barabbas as they had requested.

Pilate made a deliberate choice that he knew was wrong. He was responsible for his decision, as we are for ours. And yet we know that the Lord Jesus came to give His life to take sin's punishment for everyone who trusts in Him. We cannot fully understand how God works through all our "choices" and carries out His plans and purposes. We call this God's "sovereignty", which means that God rules over everything.

**READ: MATTHEW 26:59-67; 27:11-26; ACTS 2:23; JOHN 19:12**

**QUESTIONS:**

1. Was the trial before the Jewish council fair? (Matthew 26:59-61) What was the verdict? (Matthew 26:66)
2. What did Pilate know about the Jewish leaders? (Matthew 27:18)
3. What was Pilate afraid of? (Matthew 27:24; John 19:12)

# THE SECRET DISCIPLE WHO CHOSE TO COME FORWARD

Joseph was a member of the Jewish council. He came from the town of Arimathea which was probably a little over twenty miles north of Jerusalem. Joseph was present when the council met to put the Lord Jesus on trial before His crucifixion. He did not agree when the council decided that Jesus should be put to death. Secretly, he was a follower of Jesus, but he was afraid to make this known.

At the time of the crucifixion, even the disciples, Jesus' closest friends, were afraid of what might happen to them. But this was the time that Joseph showed that he was not like the other Jewish leaders. He knew that a great wrong had been done by the council. He determined that the body of Jesus be treated properly and with respect. He went to Pilate, the governor, and asked permission to take the body of Jesus from the cross. This was granted and he dealt with the body with help from Nicodemus, the Pharisee who had chosen to meet the Lord Jesus.

Most of the Jewish leaders hated the Lord Jesus. They hated seeing the crowds listening to Him and they hated seeing the wonderful miracles that He did. Joseph risked mockery for being known as a disciple of Jesus. The other leaders could have made his life very difficult. But just at this most difficult time, Joseph showed his love for Jesus. After using the spices that Nicodemus brought, the body was wrapped in linen and laid in a tomb in a garden.

About seven hundred years before these things happened, the prophet Isaiah wrote about them. He gave the people God's message about the promised Saviour, who would make "his grave with the wicked – but with the rich at His death" (Isaiah 53:9). The Lord Jesus was crucified with two criminals and then given a proper burial by the wealthy Joseph of Arimathea. This fulfilled exactly what Isaiah had said so long before. Isaiah Chapter 53 makes it very clear that the promised Saviour would bear the sin of all who trust in Him.

## READ: ISAIAH 53; LUKE 23:50-53; JOHN 12:42; JOHN 19:38-42
## QUESTIONS:

1. Find the verse in Isaiah Chapter 53 that includes the words that were fulfilled by Joseph and Nicodemus.
2. What was Joseph not in agreement about? (Luke 23:50-51)
3. The synagogue was very important to the Jews. It was the place where they met together and where the Old Testament scriptures were read and explained. Read John 12:42. Why do you think Joseph was a secret disciple?

# THOMAS WHO CHOSE TO DOUBT

After the Lord Jesus was crucified, the disciples were afraid of what would happen to them. They were together on the third day after the crucifixion, on the first day of the week, our Sunday. The doors were closed. Suddenly, Jesus was there with them. He told them that He brought them peace. He showed them the scars on His hands and side, so that they knew it really was Him. He had risen from the dead.

When Jesus had told His disciples that He would die and rise again, they had not understood. Now they knew that He had conquered death. He was truly the Son of God, who had come into the world to give His life so that sinners could be saved.

One disciple, Thomas, was not present when Jesus came into the room. The others told him that they had seen the Lord Jesus. Thomas said that he could only believe if he actually touched the scars on Jesus' hands and side. He had chosen to doubt that Jesus had really risen from the dead.

Eight days later, the Lord Jesus came again to His disciples. This time, Thomas was with them.

Jesus knew what Thomas had said. He invited him to see and touch His scars. Thomas answered by saying, "My Lord and my God!" He too now knew without any more doubting, that Jesus was God the Son.

The Lord Jesus told Thomas that those who believe even though they have not seen Him, are blessed. This must include everyone who has believed in the Lord Jesus, since He returned to heaven (He did this forty days after His resurrection). We can believe all that the Bible tells us about the Lord Jesus. In fact, the apostle John says that all that he wrote in his Gospel, is there so that we will believe that Jesus is the Son of God, and have life through Him.

### READ: JOHN 20
### QUESTIONS:
1. Who was the first person to see the Lord Jesus after He had risen? (John 20:1, 11-18)
2. What did Thomas say he needed to do before He would believe that the other disciples had seen the Lord Jesus? (John 20:25)
3. Why did John write about the things that Jesus had done? (John 20:30-31)

# PETER AND JOHN CHOOSE TO OBEY GOD

In the four Gospels we read about the twelve disciples whom the Lord Jesus chose to be with Him. After the Lord Jesus rose from the dead and returned to heaven, the Holy Spirit came to the disciples on the day of Pentecost (Acts Chapter 2). In the Book of Acts we find the disciples are now known as apostles – those who were sent by God to take the gospel to the people of Jerusalem, the land of Israel and then to all the world.

One day, Peter and John were at the temple in Jerusalem. They saw a man there who had been lame all his life – he could not walk. Every day he was carried to one of the gates of the temple so that he could beg from people there. Peter called on the Lord Jesus and told the man to get up and walk. As Peter helped him up, immediately the man was able to walk. Many people had seen what had happened and Peter was able to speak to them about the Lord Jesus.

Some of the priests and leaders of the people heard Peter speaking about Jesus. They imprisoned Peter and John until the next day, when they brought them in to be questioned. Peter was not afraid to tell them that the one they had crucified had risen from the dead. It was by His power that the lame man had been healed.

Peter and John had to wait while the priests and others with them decided what to do. They could not deny that a miracle had taken place, but they wanted to stop Peter and John teaching people about Jesus. They ordered them not to speak any more about Him. They threatened them about what would happen to them if they disobeyed this order.

Peter and John replied that it was a matter of whether they should obey God or obey men. They said that they must speak of all that they knew about the Lord Jesus. Jesus Himself had told them that they must be His witnesses: those who tell others what they have seen and heard.

Peter and John made their choice – they would obey God whatever threats were made against them. We can all learn from their choice. There are people that it is right to obey: our parents, our teachers and those who rule our country. But if anyone tells us to do something different from what God says we should do, we must obey God.

### READ: ACTS 1:8; ACTS 3; ACTS 4:1-22
### QUESTIONS:
1. Did Peter claim that he had healed the lame man? (Acts 3:12-16)
2. How did Peter explain to the priests what had happened? (Acts 4:10)
3. What orders did the priests give to Peter and John? What had the Lord Jesus told them to do? (Acts 4:18; 1:8)

# ANANIAS AND SAPPHIRA: A DISHONEST CHOICE

After He rose from the dead, the Lord Jesus told His disciples that they must tell people about Him, about His death on the cross and His resurrection. The early chapters of the Book of Acts tell us about things that happened after the Lord Jesus went back to heaven. We read about Peter speaking to a great crowd of people who had come to Jerusalem for the Feast of Pentecost.

Many people became Christians as they listened to the apostle's teaching. (The eleven disciples are now called apostles – "apostle" means "sent out" for a particular work.) These early Christians helped one another. Some sold their possessions so that they could give to those who were in need.

Ananias and his wife Sapphira sold some land. They agreed together that they would take some of the money to the apostles, and keep some for themselves. This was not wrong, as it was their own money. But they chose to make it appear that they were giving all the money from the sale. They chose to act dishonestly.

Ananias brought the money to the apostles. The Holy Spirit helped Peter to understand that Ananias was not being honest. Peter told him that he was lying to the Holy Spirit. Ananias wanted to be seen doing something very good, but he was showing by what he did, that he had not truly repented of his sin. A terrible thing happened. Ananias collapsed and died. Later that day, Sapphira came in. Peter asked her about the money that the land had been sold for. She gave a dishonest answer. Sapphira collapsed just as her husband had done.

Ananias and Sapphira chose to lie, and their lie had terrible consequences. To lie to another person is sinful. To lie to God is even more serious. We cannot deceive God. He knows our hearts. In this true story of Ananias and Sapphira we have a warning about how important it is to be sincere, not to pretend to be something we are not. If we truly love the Lord Jesus, we will ask Him to show us anything in our lives that is wrong. (Psalm 139:23-24)

## READ: JOHN 14:17; ACTS 5:1-11; EPHESIANS 5:9
## QUESTIONS:

1. What did Ananias and Sapphira do wrong? (Acts 5:2-4)
2. What is the Holy Spirit called in John 14:17?
3. Find three things which the Holy Spirit brings into the life of a Christian? (Ephesians 5:9)

# SAUL: WHO CHOSE TO PERSECUTE CHRISTIANS

Saul was a Pharisee. We first read about him in the Book of Acts, after the Lord Jesus had gone back to heaven. He did not believe that Jesus was the Son of God, the Saviour whom God had promised. He wanted to stop people believing in Jesus or teaching others about Him. Saul was proud to belong to the Jewish nation. He was proud of how strict he was in keeping God's law. When he began to persecute (ill-treat) Christians he thought that he was doing right.

Saul asked the High Priest to give him letters to the Jews in Damascus. This was to help him to find people who had become Christians. When they were found, they would be taken by force from their homes to Jerusalem, where it would be decided what should be done to them. (They could be put in prison or even put to death.)

However, Saul never harmed any Christians in Damascus. Something happened to him on the way, that changed his life completely. As he drew near to Damascus, a light from heaven shone around Saul and he fell to the ground. The Lord Jesus spoke and asked him why he was persecuting Him. Saul trembled as he asked what he should do. Jesus told him to go to Damascus and he would be told what to do.

When Saul stood up, he was unable to see. The men who were with him led him into the city. God sent a man named Ananias to speak to Saul. Saul's sight was restored and he was baptized. He met with other Christians at Damascus and then began to tell the people in the synagogues, that Jesus is the Son of God.

### READ: ACTS 9:1-21
### QUESTIONS:
1. Why did Saul go to see the High Priest? (Acts 9:1-2)
2. On the road to Damascus, what did he see and what did he hear? (Acts 9:3-4)
3. How did Ananias react when God told him to go to Saul? (Acts 9:13-14)
4. Instead of persecuting Christians, what did Saul do? (Acts 9:20)

# EXTRA

Saul persecuted Christians and believed that that was right. On the road to Damascus, Jesus spoke to him and his whole life changed. Years later, Saul said, "I was not disobedient to the heavenly vision" (Acts 26:19). Saul the persecutor became Paul the missionary, who travelled far to tell others about the Lord Jesus.

God had chosen Saul for a special task (Acts 9:15), just as in Old Testament times He chose Abraham, Moses and others. In a wonderful way, God carries out His plans, even in the life of Saul who had at first made a wrong choice.

The Bible tells us how to make wise choices by remembering God (Proverbs 3:5-6); to choose the way that leads to life (Deuteronomy 30:19).

When we have made a wrong choice, God will forgive us if we are truly sorry. But even God's forgiveness does not remove the consequences of what we have done. We may have caused much trouble to ourselves and others. The Bible encourages us to always ask God to help us in all the choices we make.

# FELIX: WHO CHOSE TO PROCRASTINATE

Paul travelled many miles to tell people about the Lord Jesus. When he returned to Jerusalem some Jews caused a disturbance, making false accusations against Paul. They were so angry that Paul was in danger of being killed. Lysias the commander of the Roman garrison took soldiers to put an end to the riot. Paul was taken to the barracks to be held as a prisoner.

Lysias learned that there was a plot to kill Paul. He decided to send him to Felix the Roman governor at Caesarea for his own safety.

Some Jewish leaders came to Felix to make accusations against Paul. Paul was then allowed to speak for himself. After listening to Paul, Felix said he would wait until Lysias came, before deciding what should be done.

After some days, Felix sent for Paul again. This time he listened while Paul spoke about the Lord Jesus. Felix was the governor and Paul was his prisoner and yet Felix became afraid as he listened to Paul's words.

Felix chose to procrastinate, which means that he put off thinking about his sins and the day he would meet God as his judge. Felix said that he would listen to Paul again, when it suited him. Felix thought that Paul might give him money in the hope of being set free.

Felix was not a good man. He knew that Paul was innocent of any crime. When a new governor took over from him, to please the Jews, Felix left Paul in prison. His choice to ignore what Paul had said, meant that he would one day come before God with his sins unforgiven. This is a warning to us. Do not put off asking God to forgive your sins. Trust in the Lord Jesus, who died to take sin's punishment.

### READ: ACTS 21:30-35; ACTS 24; 2 CORINTHIANS 6:2
### QUESTIONS:

1. When the Jews spoke to Felix, did they tell the truth? (Acts 21:30-35; 24:6-7)
2. What effect did Paul's words have on Felix the governor? (Acts 24:25)
3. When is it the right time to think about salvation? (2 Corinthians 6:2)

# KING AGRIPPA: WHO ALMOST MADE A RIGHT CHOICE

Festus took over from Felix as the Roman governor at Caesarea. He listened to the accusations the Jews made against Paul, as Felix had done. Paul knew that he was being treated unjustly and so he decided to appeal to Caesar Augustus (the Roman Emperor). This gave Festus a problem. He did not know what information about Paul he should send with him to the emperor.

King Agrippa came to visit Festus at Caesarea. Festus was then able to tell him about Paul. The king said that he would like to hear Paul speak for himself. So it was arranged that Paul would be brought before the king and the governor.

Paul was glad of this opportunity to speak. We can read his words in Acts Chapter 26. He not only made his own defence against his accusers, he also spoke about the Lord Jesus. After listening to all that Paul said, the king answered him, "You almost persuade me to become a Christian." King Agrippa knew that

Paul was not a criminal. He knew that Paul's words were true.

Agrippa belonged to the family of the Herods. Members of this family had carried out some very wicked actions, including the killing of little children around Bethlehem after the birth of Jesus. He was a sinful man who needed to repent and ask for God's forgiveness.

King Agrippa had heard the gospel that God's Son had come into the world, that He had died on the cross to take the punishment for the sin of everyone who trusts in Him and had risen again and ascended into heaven. This was his opportunity to repent of his sins and trust in the Lord Jesus. He let the opportunity pass. Some people think he did not take Paul's words seriously and that his words meant, "Do you really think you can persuade me to be a Christian?". But Paul took him seriously and told him how much he would like King Agrippa to become a Christian as he had done.

There is no such thing as an "almost Christian". Paul wanted all who heard him to be "altogether" convinced of the truth of his words and believe the gospel that he proclaimed.

### READ: ACTS 25:22-27; 26:1-32
### QUESTIONS:
1. Why was Festus pleased that King Agrippa was willing to hear Paul? (Acts 26:1-3)
2. How did Paul treat Christians, before he became a Christian himself? (Acts 26:9-11)
3. What did Paul say that the Old Testament taught about the promised Saviour (the Christ)? (Acts 26:22-23)

# JULIUS: THE CENTURION'S CHOICE TO SAVE PAUL

After the apostle Paul had appealed to Caesar, arrangements were made for him to travel to Rome. He was put on a ship with some other prisoners. A centurion named Julius was in charge of the prisoners.

Sailing ships faced great danger on the Mediterranean Sea, especially late in the year, the season of storms. After a stop at a place called Fair Havens, Paul warned of danger ahead, but those in charge of the ship preferred to find another port to spend the winter.

They set off and were caught in a severe storm. The crew gave up hope of being saved. Paul was calm in the storm. He told the men that an angel of God had assured him that there would be no loss of life.

The crew were encouraged by Paul, and seeing land, they decided to run the ship on to a beach. The ship stuck fast and was being broken by the waves. The soldiers planned to kill the prisoners rather than let them swim away and escape. The centurion did not allow this. He was determined to save Paul. He gave orders that those who could swim should swim to the shore. Others took boards from the ship and managed to get to land on them. All reached land and were kindly treated by the locals. They had landed on the island of Malta.

The centurion had made a brave and merciful choice. He was responsible for the prisoners and would have been in trouble if any had escaped. God had said that Paul would appear before kings. During the storm, He told Paul that he must appear before Caesar. The centurion's choice was all part of God's plan for Paul.

## READ: ACTS 27; 28:1-2
## QUESTIONS:
1. What warning did Paul give to the crew and did they take any notice? (Acts 27:9-11)
2. Why did Paul remain calm in the storm? (Acts 27:20-26)
3. What choice did the centurion make about the prisoners? (Acts 27:42-44)

# THE MOST IMPORTANT CHOICE: REVELATION 22:17

When you receive an invitation you must choose to accept or reject it. All through the Bible, we read the invitations that God has given to come to Him. The last one calls on those who are thirsty to come and "take the water of life".

We cannot live without water. Travellers in the desert tell us how terrible thirst can be. But the invitation in Revelation Chapter 22 is about a different kind of thirst – a desire for the life that God gives.

Our hearts are sinful and we do not love God, even though He has given us life and so many beautiful things to enjoy. If you feel a "thirst", a longing to know God and to have the "abundant life" that the Lord Jesus spoke of (John 10:10), it is because God is helping you to realise your need of Him.

How do we "come" to God, as our verse invites us to? We come to God when we believe what He has told us in the Bible, and do what He says. God is perfectly pure and holy, and our sin prevents us knowing Him as our Friend. The Lord Jesus, the Son of God, came into the world to take the punishment for the sin of everyone who trusts in Him. We come to God when we trust in the death of His Son being all that is needed for God to forgive our sin. The Bible says that in this way, we are reconciled to God. We know God as our Father and the Lord Jesus as our dearest Friend. When God forgives our sin and accepts us as His children, His Holy Spirit begins to work in our lives. Becoming a Christian does not make us perfect all at once. The Holy Spirit continues His work of making us more like the Lord Jesus, all through our lives.

What of those who want to live without any thought of God, those who have no "thirst" to know Him? The "choice" to reject God's invitation, means being separated from Him forever, in a place the Bible calls hell. God is the source of all goodness and joy, love and peace, beauty and order. So to be cut off from Him means being cut off from all these good things, for ever.

**READ SOME HELPFUL BIBLE VERSES: ISAIAH 53:6; JOHN 3:16; JOHN 10:27-29; JOHN 20:30-31; 1 JOHN 5:11-13.**

## ENDORSEMENTS

Our choices matter. The "big" choices grown-ups make are practiced in the thousands of little choices we make as we grow. This book can help children choose well and, most importantly, trust in the God who redeems our choices—even the bad ones—as He unfolds His beautiful plan.

**WILLIAM BOEKESTEIN, AUTHOR OF *SHEPHERD WARRIOR, A STORY FOR YOUNG READERS ABOUT ULRICH ZWINGLI***

This second volume by Jean Stapleton gives children further opportunity to be inspired or warned by biblical characters and the decisions they made. This book will reinforce the fact that everyone faces good and bad choices in life and, by God's grace, even children can find strength and courage to choose well.

**HEATHER LEFEBVRE, AUTHOR OF *THE HISTORY OF CHRISTMAS***

# Good Choices, Bad Choices

## 40 Bible Characters Decide

### Jean Stapleton

# Good Choices, Bad Choices
*40 Bible Characters Decide*
Jean Stapleton

The Bible teaches us that God always does what He says He will do. It is a great comfort to know, that God's plans and purposes are not changed by men and women who make wrong or foolish choices. In a way that we cannot understand, God rules over everything, so that His promises are always fulfilled. From the first wrong choice made by Adam and Eve throughout the Bible we meet many people who chose well or who made foolish decisions. This book will help you to focus on God's Word and His wisdom guiding you in your own day to day choices.

ISBN: 978-1-5271-0527-0

# Read with me

### 365 Family Readings Giving An Overview Of The Bible

## Jean Stapleton

# Read with Me
## by Jean Stapleton

*Read with Me* takes the stories and teachings of the Bible from the beginning of the Old Testament through to the end of the New, explaining them in simple, direct language.

These devotions are ideal for reading to children – each one bringing out truths and questions, answers and lessons – and will bring your family closer to God.

Each reading is divided up into four sections: –
- God's Word – gives you short passages of scripture to read together.
- Extra Info – teaches interesting facts about God, the Bible, and the world.
- By Myself – allows young and developing readers to tackle a sentence or two.
- Ask about it – asks questions that are easily answered from the readings.

For older family members there is also an additional feature where, throughout the book, introductions are given to those Old and New Testament books that are featured. These give useful information for older children – or for adults to read alongside the family devotions.

This book is a simple, effective way to encourage your family to come together and spend time in a daily walk with God through His Word.

ISBN: 978-1-84550-148-8

# GIRLS JUST LIKE YOU
*Bible Women who Trusted God*

JEAN STAPLETON

## Girls Just Like You
### by Jean Stapleton

We might think that people in Bible times were different from us (much braver and better than we are), but that isn't true. They were just like us – just like you, in fact!

There are fifty different stories in this book, with Bible verses to read that will teach you about the girls and women in the Bible who trusted God. Find out about them and about yourself by discovering God's Word that He has written for you!

ISBN: 978-1-78191-997-2

# BOYS JUST LIKE ME

*Bible Men who Trusted God*

JEAN STAPLETON

# Boys Just Like Me
by Jean Stapleton

We might think that people in Bible times were different from us (much braver and better than we are), but that isn't true. They were just like us – just like you, in fact!

There are fifty different stories in this book, with Bible verses to read that will teach you about the boys and men in the Bible who trusted God. Find out about them and about yourself by discovering God's Word that He has written for you!

ISBN: 978-1-78191-998-9

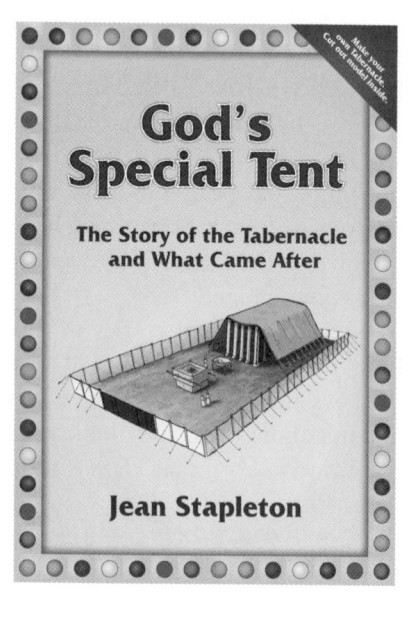

# God's Special Tent

### The Story of the Tabernacle and What Came After

Make your own Tabernacle. Cut out model inside.

**Jean Stapleton**

# God's Special Tent
## by Jean Stapleton

Do you like tents? Perhaps you've gone camping, staying in one place and then moving to another. God's people the Israelites lived in tents in the wilderness as they moved from Egypt to the Promised Land. God gave them instructions about how to make a special tent - where He could be present among His people. Find out about how they made this tent and what special furniture and curtains were placed inside it. How did they build the tent and how did they carry it from one place to another? The priests made sacrifices to atone for the sin of the people, but the tabernacle or tent of meeting was a place that taught the people about the one who was going to save them from their sin for good - Jesus Christ, the promised Messiah. His sacrifice would mean that no other sacrifices were needed and that people could worship God all around the world.

ISBN: 978-1-84550-811-1

# Fascinating Bible Facts Vol. 1
## by Irene Howat

How about going on a fact-finding expedition? This journey will take you into the past and the future by introducing you to the magnificent, amazing, fascinating Bible!

There are some surprising stories in God's Word about animals, trees and forests, and families – amongst other things. In *Fascinating Bible Facts Vol. 1*, you will find out about the beginning of time, but also discover the most amazing place that ever was or will be – heaven!

Each of the devotions has a Bible promise for you to read. Throughout the book, find out the questions Chloe has for you to answer, the facts that Abbi has for you to learn, and the activities that Zac has for you to do.

ISBN: 978-1-5271-0143-2

# Fascinating Bible Facts Vol. 2
## by Irene Howat

How about going on a fact–finding expedition? This journey will take you into the past and the future by introducing you to the magnificent, amazing, fascinating Bible!

Discover the names of Jesus and what the word 'Bible' means while following the life of Jesus from His birth through to His death and resurrection.

Each of the devotions has a Bible Promise for you to read. Throughout the book, find out the questions Chloe has for you to answer, the facts that Abbi has for you to learn, and the activities that Zac has for you to do.

ISBN: 978-1-5271-0144-9